Dedicated to my children—my world.

Foreword

Alcoholism has been a well-known problem for centuries but has never been viewed or addressed as a Jewish problem. There exists a myth that Jewish people do not drink, use illicit drugs and are not alcoholics or drug addicts. As a Jew I believe that the time is now for my people to have a rude awakening and face the facts.

The Jewish people have their share of alcoholics and drug addicts as all other ethnic groups have in the world. I address this book to all the parents, teachers, religious leaders, alcoholics and addicts who must face the realization of the growing need for the freedom from substance abuse.

My book, *The Road to Recovery*, is my story about being an alcoholic and living in my Jewish world and how I recovered. As a woman I had double fold problem. I am female and Jewish. Criticized by my family and friends for my alcoholic behavior I was desperately despondent and thought I had nowhere to turn. Gratefully, Alcoholic's Anonymous became my salvation.

Through the AA program and a loving support system from my friends and family I found a path and a code of ethics I could live by. Hopefully, people will read my story and gather faith from it.

My story is full of woe and recrimination for which there was a simple solution. It was just a question of finding it.

The Road to Recovery

I stood on a high cliff looking down at a river of booze hoping I would die. I wanted to stop drinking but I could not do it alone. With the help of my children and Alcoholic's Anonymous I was able to take my first steps back to reality. This is the story of one woman's leap from inebriation to sobriety. Having lost serenity and spirituality I was able to find my way back to God. It was not an easy step. The abyss is wide.

Chapter I

It's a myth that Jewish woman are not alcoholics. (Or men, for that matter.) I am Jewish and I am an Alcoholic. Jewish women like all other women, despite their religious denomination, are apt to have any or all the shortcomings, diseases, or mental problems that other women have. We are not unique. We just don't talk about the alcoholic cousin we have stashed away in the closet. It would be a "shanda" (an embarrassment) to admit having a drunken mother, aunt or grandmother. Jewish women are supposed to be the models of propriety. The Jewish moral code supposedly sets the rules and standards for women in the Jewish society. When Moses set down the laws I think he should have reflected upon his own sister, realized her vulnerability and considered the possibilities of characteristic flaws in all humans.

Moses, Aaron, and Miriam were the leaders of the wandering Hebrews. Miriam had the bad judgment of criticizing, Zipporah, the wife of Moses. Speaking ill of her because of her skin color and stating that she was from a foreign tribe Miriam wanted her disposed of. It is written that God heard Miriam and as punishment instantly inflicted her with leprosy. She was exiled outside of the encampment until she rescinded her remarks. When she was returned to the flock there was a wild celebration. Miriam put on her ankle bells, shook her tambourine, sang, danced and embraced Zipporah. All was forgiven. I drank, I sang, I danced and I drank some more. I think of myself as Miriam exiled into the desert. Perhaps, I have been forgiven, as well.

I believe that when Moses wrote *Deuteronomy* he did not take into account the modernization of women. He could not have foreseen the pressures in our modern society. Let us look at today's Jewish woman. She is probably educated and has at least a master's degree in something. She has a profession where she earns big dollars. Perhaps, she is married but if not has a well decorated apartment, designer clothes and lives alone or has a live-in partner—male or female. There is a big chance that she is a single mom either having adopted a baby, had artificial insemination, or promiscuous sex, all with her family's blessings. In biblical times (or Nigeria) she would have been stoned. In reality, this woman stones herself by getting "stoned", and becomes an alcoholic.

My story is not different from many other Jewish women. My family was secular Jews. The holy holidays were all celebrated. My mother kept a kosher kitchen. My father donned the prayer shawl and phylacteries every morning to pray. We did not keep the Sabbath except for the Friday night meal where Sabbath candles were lit and a prayer given.

As for religious training, only the boys were sent to the rabbi for religious instruction. Girls? We did what our mothers taught us. Mostly it was kitchen duties so that we would know how to prepare kosher food. Ideally, a girl would marry, have children, grandchildren and carry on tradition.

They forgot two things. One, I became a modern, educated woman and two; I inherited the disease of alcoholism. Everything was fine until life and its problems became too much to handle. It took a lot of effort for me to visit a rabbi and admit that I had a drinking problem. When I finally summoned enough courage I found a rabbi that didn't know me. I didn't say that I was an alcoholic but meekly said that I was having a problem and that I was drinking too much. He told me that it was very un-Jewish and told me to stop but he didn't tell me how.

My father, two grandfathers, my aunts and uncles were all alcoholics. My mother and one aunt were the only two sober people in the family. Actually, I didn't drink until I was thirty-five then I developed a love affair with alcohol. My marriage was drifting along on a stagnant pond. Actually, looking back I realize that I was emotionally abused and had become the "Okay" girl. Whatever my husband said I said, "Okay." His friends became my friends but he would not accept my friends. He would never accept my complaints, ideas or needs. The fault was not his alone. I should have objected but I was too busy. I had a job, a house to take care of that included shopping and cleaning, a husband, two kids, a dog, a bird, a turtle and two mothers. I am an artist and sculptor. I sometimes worked late into the night, as it was the only time I found time for myself. It was about that time that I started to drink.

And, I did have a job. I was a fashion designer for children's clothes. It was glamorous, creative, demanding, and it put me in with a group of people who were high flyers. Fashion shows parties, always with martinis close at hand. After work there was always the bus home to reality. I compared it to an elevator ride; soaring to the top floor and then plunking down to rock bottom.

I would come home from work and pour a large shot of vodka and drink while preparing dinner. Load the dishwasher and rush off to the nursing home to tend my mother and prepare her for the night. Rush home to throw in a wash and then help the boys with their homework. I would descend to the basement, my studio, to work on an ongoing creation, usually with the bottle of vodka, trying to fight off the wild decent. Many a night I would climb the stairs to the darkened house. My husband was an insomniac and usually went to bed about 9:00 with two sleeping pills. Needless to say our relationship was nothing.

My mother had a stroke and was paralyzed on her left side. She had many reoccurring accidents that finally had her spend her remaining days in a nursing home. My mother-in-law suffered from what we now know as Alzheimer's disease and eventually had to have supervised care. My husband chose to remain oblivious to our mothers' conditions and I was their main caregiver.

My boys were my only consolation in my life. They were healthy, athletic, and active. Again, my husband did not participate in our activities. I cheered them at Little League, helped them with their homework, introduced them to books and poetry, helped them with their hobbies, and taught them about nature and the world around us. I enjoyed my children and was dedicated to them. I really was a single mom. It paid off. My children were the people that intervened and led me into recovery.

All of the above are poor reasons to drink. I went on drinking feeling sorry for myself. I went to a psychiatrist and after telling my story he told me to get a divorce. It was just another reason to drink. So I thought. I did not try to solve my problems. Drinking was more enjoyable and easier. I fantasized constantly about how to escape. When the situation presented itself I found a boyfriend. Not only had I lost my spirituality, now I was committing adultery.

It was a Saturday afternoon and I went to visit my mother at the nursing home. I was shocked to find her in a coma attached to machines and tubes. Hysterically, I asked the nurses why they were trying to save her. I called my husband and he said, "Does that mean we won't be going for dinner?" I called my brother. He told me to call me when she was dead. I called my best friend and she said they were just leaving for an appointment and would see me in the morning. She never asked me why I was calling.

The woman that shared the room with my mother kept screaming, "Is she dead yet?"

I returned home and got dressed in my best outfit, mink coat and diamond earrings. Knocked back a couple of straight vodkas and went back to the nursing home and hoped my mother would open her eyes just once and see me in my finery. She never could or would. I told the nurses to pull the plugs.

I sat by my mother's side for a long time reflecting upon my own life. Inwardly, I experienced the primal scream. Outwardly, I was numb.

Right after the funeral I told my husband that I wanted a divorce. He just didn't get it. He thought we had the perfect marriage.

Psychiatrists talk about a person having a nervous breakdown. Looking back, now, I believe that I had a doozie! I had put all of my mother's and mother-in-law's belongings, furniture and all into our garage and had a garage sale. One morning when I looked into the garage I thought, "Is this all there is to a person's life? An ashtray, a dish? What's in my life?" I believe I snapped. I wanted to run away. I was worn out from taking care of people. Of course, I couldn't run from my responsibilities. I had children and a job. I had a tall Queen Anne wing chair in my living room and it became my retreat. I didn't want to clean the house, do the wash, or cook. I took a leave of absence from my work and settled into the chair with a glass of vodka in my hand.

I told my husband he could have the house and that I didn't want any of his money. Certainly, no alimony. I wanted to be free of him. In our divorce agreement I insisted that he had to hire a housekeeper until the boys were 21. I packed my antiques into cartons and marked each one with a boy's name for when they would marry and have homes of their own. And I left. Packed my car with my personal belongings, left the key to the house on the kitchen table with a note for my husband: "You put out the garbage."

Chapter II

If you are going to be an alcoholic, New York is the perfect place. I still had the glamorous job and rented an apartment in the fashionable part of New York with a view of the Hudson River. My boyfriend moved in with me but that didn't last too long. I didn't give up my drinking and he had a drug habit that I couldn't cope with. My social life became bars and one-night stands. I was, however, a functional alcoholic: Did my job well and rewarded myself each evening with a good stiff drink or two or three or four…

About that time I started looking for answers but didn't realize I had to ask questions first before I could get answers. I was not happy in my new life and again looked for escape. My older son was living in Israel and he knew how unhappy I was. He wrote two and three letters a day telling me to visit. Finally, I did. I went for two weeks and stayed sixteen years. I was employed as the fashion director of a very large textile company and again I was in the social whirl. Both locally, and internationally. I traveled a great deal for the company and drank in Tel Aviv, Paris, Florence, Munich, London and New York. I still didn't think that I had a problem.

By this time I was 62 years old and decided to retire. I returned to the States and settled into retirement. Now I was a grandmother and still an alcoholic. It was a dark and stormy family night and my daughter-in-law said, "If you don't stop drinking you will never see your grandchildren again!" Those words were enough to get me sober. I agreed to go to a rehabilitation center for recovery.

Of course, I did exactly the thing that one should not do. I stopped drinking and dried out on my own. By the end of the first week my teeth were chattering, my hands were shaking and I had the D.T.'s. I could have died but didn't. Still believing that I could do it on my own I drove myself to Hazelden in West Palm Beach. I could not get it through my thick head how I was going to recover, reform, or anything else in 28 days? It was not until I heard that alcoholism is a disease that I began to see a ray of hope. Having the disease was one thing but controlling it was another. Some people have diabetes and they control it with medication and eating the proper food. I knew there was no medication for alcoholism. The only control for it was to stop drinking.

Could it be that I had inherited my alcohol problem from my father and grandfathers.

I began to wonder about my sanity. Where was my self-control? I knew that I had to stop blaming others and pretending. I did not want to lose my children and grandchildren. Drinking was messing up my life and hurting those that I loved and those who loved me. I knew that I had to stop trying to take this major step alone. I had to be willing to take the first step by myself and admit that I was an alcoholic. My recovery began when I gave up on denial and admitted to being powerless over alcohol.

The Jewish faith teaches that we can be forgiven for our sins and that every day is a new day. Thankfully, I still had a hint of spirituality left within me and I wondered if I could ask for forgiveness. I needed to find a life raft as I drifted in the sea of confusion. There I was; clinging to a bit of flotsam and hoping I could stay afloat.

There were sixteen other woman in our group of different ages. There was one woman older than myself and I felt relieved. One would think that at our age we would know better. Alcohol has no age limit. It is sly and cunning. The first drink might make you feel good but if you are an alcoholic one drink is too much and a bottle is not enough.

Everybody has a story to tell. We call them "War Stories." Some stories are worse then others. As I told my story I realized how angry I was. I knew that I had to rid myself of the anger before I could heal. One of my counselors was a Catholic priest (a recovering alcoholic). I was immediately able to relate to him. I knew that he had knowledge of many religions and could understand me. One of my major issues was the death of my parents. I had been close to both of them and I would not accept their death. I could not bury the past. He advised that I write letters to them and then bury or burn the letters. I told my father that I loved him but that I had resented having to be the caretaker in the family. I asked why he had given me so much responsibility at such a young age. I wanted to know why I was designated to care for my aunts when they had babies. Why I had to stop my education to help him in the business. Why he had died at such a young age leaving me to take care of my mother. I was blaming someone else for my problem.

I wrote to my mother and told her that she was my best friend and I didn't want her to die. After I wrote the letters and burned them I felt released. Soon after, I had a dream about my parents. I believe I transcended and could see them at a Passover table with all of our family. The words from the story of the Passover were being read; we were strangers in the land. We were slaves. When I awoke I knew that I had been a slave to alcohol and now I was a stranger struggling to find my way. The dream and the letters made me feel better and some of the tension was released.

The priest at Hazelden was by far the most sympathetic and helpful person that I have met in my recovery. During one session of my time spent with him we discussed the issue of ethnic values. If someone were to say, "I'm Irish and I'm an alcoholic," everyone in the room seems to snicker. If a person says, "I'm Jewish and I'm an alcoholic," eyebrows are raised.

Why is alcoholism synonymous with being Irish and Judaism is not? Perhaps, it is because the Irish drink at pubs and Jews drink at home. Closet drinking is not unusual but Jews are coming out of the closet since younger Jewish people are frequenting clubs and bars.

The priest at Hazelden agreed that this was often the case.

To my great surprise he gave me an AA *Haggadah*. The *Haggadah* is the book with the story of Exodus, the Jewish story of Moses leading the Hebrews out of Egypt and conducting a Seder. The Seder is the traditional yearly meal that celebrates the Exodus. During the Seder many glasses of wine are consumed. In the AA *Haggadah* grape juice replaces the wine.

I was very touched by his offering and impressed about how realistic Alcoholics Anonymous had become.

Chapter III

I was part of a small group of women each with a story to tell. When it was my turn to speak I began with, "I drank a river of booze." I believed it to be true. I envied the young women in the group who had found the right path to sobriety at a young age and would have a new chance before they messed up their lives the way I did. I had deluded myself into believing that I could control my own life. Suddenly, I knew that I was terrified of not being in control and that I was powerless over alcohol. It was then that I reflected on a higher power. Something? Someone? God?

My thoughts went to the Jewish people and how powerless they were when they were forced out of their homes in countless generations. They had to take a first step in order to survive. Some had their lives restored to them. I wanted my life to be restored. I wanted order in my life. Perhaps, that is why I functioned in my work. There is a big part of me that respects and wants order. However, at that moment I was feeling anger and guilt. I was angry with my children for forcing me into a recovery center and I was guilty about the things I had done and said during my drunken bouts.

When I heard the other stories I began to think that my story wasn't so bad. Most of the women had begun their drinking careers while in their teens. I was a late bloomer. I began to think just how lucky they were to be able to change their lives while they were still young. They could begin a new day and start afresh.

Loretta, a petite blonde with pretty green eyes told us she was twenty-eight years old and had started to drink when she was twelve. When her mother entertained she would share a beer with her mother's boyfriend. The boyfriend thought it was funny. When the parties were over and mother and boyfriend retreated to the bedroom, Loretta would drink whatever was left in the glasses.

She loved the intoxicated feeling and soon started nipping from the liquor cabinet on her own. Soon after, at the ripe old age of fifteen, she had her own boyfriend and together they would skip school, drink beer and smoke marijuana. After mother and boyfriends she found she could not support herself and became a prostitute. Loretta had been ordered by the courts to enter a detox center. I knew from listening to her that as soon as the 28 days were over she would be on the street again.

Sheila, another beautiful woman, could hardly tell her story without crying.

She was divorced and her husband had custody of the children. She had visiting rights but her husband had taken the children to live in California and she was stuck in Florida. Whenever she had thought about traveling she drank and was too sick to travel. Of course, she couldn't be sure she wouldn't drink once she arrived in California.

Vicki, a young woman from Ohio arrived at the center with her leg in a cast. While driving drunk she crashed into a tree, totaled the car, causing her to almost lose her leg.

The bone in her leg was replaced with a steel rod. She still had four operations to look forward to. Vicki and I stayed in touch for a while after we left the center but eventually lost contact. I hope she made it!

I entered the recovery center and had to spend two days in detox even though I had already begun the process. Another woman that entered Hazelden with me could not stand upright. She crawled around on her hands and knees. She was not physically impaired; she was drunk. The police had found her asleep in the gutter. She became a part of our group and when she told her story she had no recollection of how she had arrived at Hazelden.

In detox my handbag and traveling case were searched for medications, drugs, weapons, or hazardous materials. I had brought vitamin pills with me that were confiscated, as something besides vitamins could have been mixed in. The center dispensed all necessary medications under the supervision of a nurse. My five medications and six vitamins had to be swallowed in front of the nurse. For me it was a fifteen-minute affair.

I was assigned to a room to be shared with another woman near to my age. The room was furnished sparely: two single beds, two dressers, a large closet, a bathroom, and no telephone. A pay phone was in the hall. We were responsible for making out own beds and keeping it clean. Every morning at 7 a.m., a volunteer from our group would awaken everybody by knocking on the door. All meals were served in the cafeteria. Breakfast at 8, classes and prayer at 9. Certainly not a luxury hotel.

My roommate, Joyce, was a hell raiser. She wore eccentric clothing and acted the part of a dizzy blonde. This was to be her sixth attempt at getting sober. She was also Jewish. Actually, there were seven Jewish women in the program with me. (So much for the myth.)

Joyce was as crazy as a bed bug! She was also a shop-o-holic. She would make phone calls to catalog shopping centers in the middle of night and order clothing. Before long her counselor put an end to packages being delivered. Joyce told me that she had tried to stop drinking but it was too much without help. She showed me a map of her backyard at home, where she had bottles of booze buried. She couldn't wait to get home. Usually, on weekends family and friends were allowed to visit. Joyce told me that her husband would be visiting. I was anxious to see him and find out what kind of a person he was. Once I met him I realized why Joyce drank. He was rude to her and very annoyed. He told me that their children did not want Joyce to be near their children. She was always drunk and exhibited behavior that was not acceptable. He also said that he believed that Joyce could not be healed since this was her fourth rehab. Actually, he had decided that there was no hope for her. He said that her shopping sprees were so excessive that he had cancelled all of her credit cards. I wondered how surprised he was going to be when he received the bill for one card that he had obviously missed. I asked him if he noticed how red and inflamed Joyce's legs were and that I thought she had phlebitis. His response was, "Who cares!"

I immediately had a reverse reaction to Joyce's craziness and her husband's unsympathetic attitude. I was there to recover. I promised to meet with her after we finished our 28 days but I knew I never would.

Parts of my being made me respond to being able to follow instructions. Once given an assignment, I was going to follow it. We were given books and told to read certain chapters and write commentary. I tried very hard to write about why I was an alcoholic but ended up in tears, angry and feeling very sorry for myself. I had the books, I listened to the lectures, I took part in all of the therapy sessions. I decided to return to the basics and found myself a Bible. I immersed myself into biblical stories and looked for God. I imagined that being in rehab was very much like being in jail. It took me awhile to realize that the recovery center was my path to freedom. That drinking was jail.

I had a few choices. I could stop drinking and go to AA meetings. I knew that I could not do it alone. I needed support. AA gives me that support. AA is a simple program and I knew it was all up to me. I think one can pray to God for help but I kept thinking about the story of the man who wanted to win the lottery and every day he prayed to God to let him win it. Week after week he lost and finally in desperation he said, "God, why don't you let me win the lottery?"

God answered: "Harry, buy a ticket!"

And so it goes with AA. Go for it!

Chapter IV

My personality and upbringing made me uncomfortable thinking that I was not responsible for what was happening to me and that I could be saved by something or someone outside of myself. I wondered what that power could be. My religion taught us that we could question and make choices. I often questioned, "Is there a God." Religion was one thing and spirituality another. I knew that I enjoyed the holidays and rituals but it had been a long time since I had prayed and I don't remember ever asking God for anything. I knew that I had been blessed with a good physical being, health and reason. It was up to me to use the tools. I was close to nature and marveled at the earth's beauty. I think that I believed in an energy force rather than a god.

In my heart I was still rebelling. I wanted desperately to replace the alcohol with something but I didn't know what. What was out there for me? Could there possibly be a God? Could God be there for me? I certainly felt a spiritual presence. How else could I have traveled so far—and who put the people who cared for me in my path? Why was my life being saved? Did I have a future mission to fulfill that I was not aware of? Did God have other plans for me? Yes, God. I had nothing else.

As a child I was required to recite prayers and I tried to remember what the prayers were. It was hopeless. I ended by saying, "God help me," over and over again. The serenity prayer became my mantra. (God, grant me the serenity to accept the things I cannot change. The courage to change the things I can and the wisdom to know the difference.) My mind was in utter confusion. It seemed that my heart was constantly racing. I yearned for serenity and peace of mind.

When I lived in Israel I met six young people either in places that I lived or through my work. They were children with big problems. Some were American, one Israeli and one from England. For some reason they leaned towards me for emotional help. They had left their families or their families had discarded them, and I represented the mother figure to them.

I helped them financially, or supplied a place for them to live, or guided their lives back to school. Some lived with me, off and on. Reflecting on those times I thought I had done a good deed. Now I know that I had nothing to do with it. God had these problem kids and needed someone to help Him. He put them on my doorstep like wet kittens, and without knowing why I took them in. Today they are all successful, with families of their own and still refer to me as mother.

Today, in recovery, I know that I had nothing to do with it. I was merely the instrument. From that moment of truth

I had found my higher power. Now all that I had to do was to regain my sanity. I know now that God trusted me. When I began the program I truly believed that I had committed so many wrongs that I would never be able to have the respect or trust of other people. I didn't understand that I was about to build a new way of life.

It has always been my habit to rise very early. Every day I would be the first and only one awake. The mornings in Florida were beautiful and I found that I could communicate with the natural setting. I could easily imagine God just by watching the birds, trees and flowers. It became a haven for me just to sit in the garden and feel the energy around me. One morning my reverie was interrupted by a woman that I recognized as being one of the counselors. She introduced herself as Sister Mary.

Sister Mary had been a nun but left the convent because of her alcoholism. She told me that when she couldn't get alcohol she would drink the vanilla in the kitchen. She asked if I would like to pray with her. I told her that I wasn't Catholic and our prayers wouldn't match. I didn't know that prayer—any prayer—would help me. Besides, we began our morning with a prayer that I half mumbled and that was enough praying for me. The prayer did not include the things that I felt in the garden. Then breakfast—we were encouraged to eat a big breakfast. I began to wonder if food was supposed to replace the alcohol. Would food replace my anger, as well?

I told myself not to think. Just do what they tell you to

do. There had to be a method to all of this process. I had heard the success stories. I only had 25 more days to complete the transformation and miracle. I started to read and as an assignment I had to write an essay about my alcoholic illness. As I read what I had written I realized it was a miracle; I had admitted that I was an alcoholic and that I was beginning to communicate my higher power again.

Chapter V

Step 3 was a revelation. I made a decision to turn my will and my life over to the care of God as I understood Him.

I read Step 3 over and over until my mind and body were numb. As much as I would like to think that I could go it alone, I knew that I had been a complete flop and needed support. I would accept God and see how it went. The first thing that came to mind was how these people came into my life to help me. Who put them there? I was beginning to believe that there was no such thing as coincidence. Was it fate or a strange higher power? It was an eerie feeling. Was someone actually watching over me? I began to feel a presence that I could not understand but I liked the feeling.

The Buddhists believe that God is a part of them. It is a concept that I can understand. I truly liked my Jewish religion. I knew that I had a forgiving God. It is true that I had forsaken my God but I was more than ready to return to the fold. Part of me wanted to be that innocent child again and I was grateful. I began my day by praying and asking God to forgive me. I ended each day with a prayer. I did not get on my knees. I believed that God could hear my prayers from wherever I happened to be. My spiritual being was standing right next to me or at times engulfing me.

Perhaps, I was becoming illusionary. I was leaving the person I was, to become the person that I wanted to be. I discussed this with my counselor and was told that it was part of recovery. I still had my doubts but I wanted to believe. I believed that God would help me to have a regular life. I knew that each day that I spent free of my addiction that I would grow stronger. Somehow I would earn the respect of my family and friends. I needed God to help me.

When our group met again for another therapy session I remained quiet. I wanted to hear the other war stories and to know how others were coping. There were several atheists in the group and listening to their stories was disturbing to me. I had moments of doubt and I wanted to speak. I wondered if the new presence that I was feeling was a figment of my imagination. Would I feel something different tomorrow? If I explained my new sensation of having had a spiritual awakening, would I be ridiculed?

I knew the stories in the Bible of how Moses had spoken to God and I had also read about when God gave the Torah. No bird sang or flew, no ox bellowed, the angels did not fly, and all was still. The sea was calm, no creature spoke. The world was still and silent when the divine voice said, "I am Adonai, your God." I believe that at that moment my world was being created. Something inside of me told me to be silent. I hope it was an inner wisdom.

Silently I prayed: Let me do the will of God with a perfect heart and a willing soul, even if it is difficult. It was the best I could come up with at the moment.

At Hazelden everyone is assigned a counselor. Mary M introduced herself as a recovering alcoholic. She had been corresponding with my son through phone calls and letters, expecting my arrival. Our first meeting was a disaster.

I was very rebellious and she was ready for me. I did not want or need a counselor. I accused her of being overly righteous. So I thought. I clung to my—I can do this myself—attitude.

First, she assigned to me a list of books and readings, including the *Alcoholic Big Book*. I was to read several chapters and make a written report. When my eyes told her that I was not about to cooperate, she told me how very upset my son was with me. She might just as well have put a knife through my heart. You might say she played dirty knowing where my soft spot was. We were to meet twice a week. Nothing I was going to look forward to.

That meeting was followed by a series of tests, including an IQ test. The tests are given when you are sober enough to take them. Statistics show that most alcoholics have IQ's over 150. If we are so smart, how come we end up in a rehab center with other drunks? I enjoyed the tests because I am a natural game player. Happiness is a crossword puzzle.

And, don't forget the shrink. He decided that I am a manic-depressive. I can't imagine why? I always explained my dual personality with the fact that I am a Gemini. Seriously, I wondered how he could evaluate me. I had been sober for a week. My mind was rattled, my nerves raw, and my tolerance to being asked questions very low. I do remember telling him to interview me in 28 days.

He wanted to prescribe a nerve medication but I was already taking Paxil to calm my mood swings. (I did try his medication and it sent me into shock and the infirmary.) I wondered what kind of a report he would be sending to my counselor, but honestly I didn't care.

Chapter VI

Step 4 said we were to make a fearless inventory of ourselves. What a fearsome step! Maybe I could skip this one. Compared to Step 4 the other steps were easy. I was the cowardly lion and this step was going to take a great deal of courage. My first question was: did I really want to change? If I could list my shortcomings I would list my favorable characteristics too.

Holding a mirror up to one's mind is not easy. The first thing that came to my mind was what an impatient person I am. I want everything done yesterday. Actually, I would rather do something myself than to give it to someone else to do because I knew they would take too long to do it or wouldn't do it right. I was impatient with friends, children and coworkers, never thinking about what they thought of me.

I also had a bad habit of wanting to make everything come out right and would invent stories or outright lie to avoid confrontation. I knew that I needed to be more honest if it didn't hurt other people.

And like Scarlet O'Hara, I had to stop putting off until tomorrow what I could do today—stay sober.

One day we were taken to an AA meeting. My first

meeting and I never thought it would become my way of life. The place was packed. One person after another stood and said, "My name is…and I am an alcoholic…" and related their story. I shuddered to think that I was going to have to do that out loud and to other people. If I really wanted to stay sober I would have to attend meetings and share my story. I played all that had happened to me over and over in my head. All I needed was courage.

With great trepidation I completed the 28 days. I had a good feeling about my self and was willing to start my new way of life. I had a booklet with all of the AA meetings listed in my area and was ready to start. I was determined to do exactly as I was told. Thankfully, I am a person that follows orders. Without directions or the support of AA I could not have survived. I attended 90 meetings for 90 days and at each one it became easier and easier to share.

At the AA meetings I found camaraderie—caring people willing to share their time and concern for me. Eventually, I learned to give back. I volunteered to make coffee, clean up after the meeting, lead a meeting—to share whenever I could.

For the first 3 years I attended a meeting every day. AA became my home away from home. During that time I found myself a sponsor. Anita was an older person who had been in the program for 26 years. I believed her to have enough wisdom and integrity to guide me through the Steps. She agreed to be my temporary sponsor, which meant that if our relationship didn't work out I wouldn't feel guilty about changing.

We began by going through the 12 Steps. I tried to tell her that I had done the Steps at Hazelden but she said we had to do them over again (and, over and over—probably forever). When we finally reached Step 5 and I had to admit to God, myself and to another human being the exact nature of my wrongs, I became caught in the confessional web again. I jokingly told Anita to get her tape recorder because my story could become a best seller.

Although, I had told myself, Anita, and other people that the biggest wrong I had committed was deserting my children. The admission did not make me feel any less guilty.

Anita told me that I had to forgive myself. Easier said than done! I saw myself as selfish and mindless and buried in guilt. I could not turn back the years or undo the things that I had done. I could only go forward and ask forgiveness. My children became adults and had their own life experiences. They came to understand and I hope they have forgiven me. I tried to talk to my ex-husband but he did not want to listen. There was nothing left for me to do except try to forgive him. I apologized to my friends for all of the late telephone calls and name-calling. They loved me and forgave me. I was elated at their response. I felt good about myself, better than I had for a long time.

The only problem I had was when family and friends told me how proud they were of me—I was embarrassed and felt childlike. Proud of me, that I could stop drinking? Proud of me that I was no longer an embarrassment? They could actually take me out in public and I would not make a scene. I could suddenly see the roles being reversed when the parent becomes the child. They would make sure I would behave. I hated them! I was the mother and they had better never forget it! Of course, I know now that it was the only way they could treat me since I had been acting like a spoiled child. Outwardly I cowered to their every wish and demands. Inwardly, I boiled!

During this time I began to wonder if God would forgive me. I did not expect an answer but I had to ask if my faithlessness and failure to believe could be overlooked. My faith teaches that God forgives and that I could return to the fold. While reflecting on Judaism and other religions I found that the key word seemed to be enlightenment and like a detective I quickly got on the trail. After many readings it all boiled down to spirituality. How much did I really believe and what did I trust?

Well, I believed in angels. The Bible talked about angels. Abraham was told by an angel not to sacrifice Isaac, Moses saw an angel arise out of the burning bush, Jacob wrestled an angel, Sara was told by an angel that she would give birth to a son. Ezekiel's experience was much more terrifying. He saw four angels that breathed fire.

I had angels. They seemed to pop up everywhere. On a plane when I was too tired to carry my own bag, a kind man realized my condition and carried it for me. Lost in a strange city, a kind person led me to my destination. Angels are really messengers of God that carry out God's work plans. In Hebrew angels are called "Amalachim." Obviously, there is a place for them in Judaism or there would not be a name for them. God needed me and I needed God.

As for enlightenment, I discovered that there are no techniques that one must follow. Inner peace comes from the self. I meditated often and not in any one special place. I think that I can compare the process to daydreaming or escaping in one's mind away from the happening of the moment. I became well trained in how to stop my mind. If we must learn in a practiced way, we will waste our time and become discouraged. We have to learn our own words and our own way of practicing. We must be sincere. We must be able to let go of the old ideas and to stay focused on the present whether we are alone, with family and friends, or at work.

While I meditated my mind did not always stay quiet and peaceful. At first, my thoughts would stray. Often, I would think about my parents. My mother could always deal with her problems and she seemed to be able to solve any situation that might present itself. My father, however, was another story. He was a peaceful and quiet man and I know that he submerged himself in prayer, yet, he constantly would become depressed. Perhaps, it was his drinking problem. I was too young to understand and I wish now that I could talk to him about it. My parents married at a very young age and there is a big chance that he never was able to fulfill his dreams leading to his depression.

Very often my mind would wander to the attitude my friends had about me. They were good friends who had never given up on me. They were all supportive and very happy that I had finally announced I had entered the AA program. In fact, at times I thought that they made too much of the situation. It was embarrassing.

It was only when I cleared my mind of the ensuing storm of events that I was able to focus on meditation. The road back was no longer an option. The road ahead was my new way of life. I was determined not to look back even though Step 5 was my stumbling block.

Step 5 was nightmare alley. My sponsor assured me that it happened to everybody who had the integrity and willingness to live up to their commitment. I had buried the guilt and now it was surfacing. I asked God to help me. I recalled the days in Jerusalem when I would visit The Wall and place small notes written to God. It is believed that an angel retrieves the notes that people place in The Wall and delivers them to God. I hope it is true. My wishes were always for health and peace. Part of my meditation takes me to Jerusalem and I visualize The Wall, lean my head against the stone and search for serenity.

Chapter VII

When I became sober I found that my life had changed. I no longer had the same friends or rather the same acquaintances. My barroom buddies no longer existed. I also found that I could read my poetry to an audience while sober. I didn't need that ego fortifying drink that I thought I needed. However, I was not writing poetry or painting, for that matter. I believed and was afraid that I had lost the magic. I honestly thought that when I drank I could reveal the images from my inner soul.

While I drank my paintings were dark and foreboding. The canvasses were too huge and I would paint and drink as if I was in a marathon. There were times when I would paint for hours at a time, until I would collapse from weariness or drink.

The poetry I wrote had the messages of the primal scream. I found no satisfaction in either the painting or the poetry.

After I became sober it took me two years before I once again found the inspiration to paint or write. The canvasses became smaller and my colors were vivid and bright. The poetry showed signs of hope.

About that time I began to have alcoholic dreams. One

dream that I remember was totally insane. It seems that I was in the supermarket and they had whiskey on sale. I ran home to get more money so that I could buy a large supply. When I returned to the market the sign was gone and no longer applied. I became frantic when I realized that I could not purchase whiskey. I awoke in a cold sweat. I have had other alcoholic dreams but fortunately, I don't remember them.

I have many friends who are poets or painters but one extremely talented artist stands out in my mind. My friend Ann who was a hopeless cross addicted drug addict and alcoholic. She was also a very talented designer and artist. When she looked at my new work she suggested that I either start drinking again or design greeting cards. I did not appreciate the criticism. How could I tell her that I was finding my way back to being a normal person when she was so dysfunctional?

Ann had her own design company that she used to support her habit. She recklessly spent money on clothes, jewelry, cars, men and cocaine. The day came when her clients were no longer interested in her work. Her brain was drugged out and so was her creativity. Her business fell off considerably. I suggested a detox center but she said that she was in control of her habit. One day one of the men that she hadn't paid for her "fix" beat her so badly she had to be hospitalized.

I sat at Ann's hospital bed through the night and in the morning called her mother. Her mother, father, the police and I, had her moved to a detox center. Ann healed but as soon as she was released she went back to using drugs. Now she sits in a place, an empty shell, nodding and sleeping. She doesn't know where she is or who she is. Her brain is burnt out. The doctors say she will never recover. Her mother goes to church every day to light a candle, as if prayer could bring her daughter back. Ann's mother has a higher power and it is that higher power that gives her hope. Ann's mother also has tremendous regrets and constantly asks, "What if?"

Ann grew up in a house where social drinking was very acceptable. Her family was members of the country club set and most weekends were spent partying. Before dinner was served the family had their cocktail hour. Ann's father always let Ann sample his drink. He thought it was cute. What they didn't know was when they were off to their club, Ann would help herself to the liquor cabinet and she acquired a taste for alcohol. Soon after, she acquired the same desire for illicit drugs. Ann had an addictive personality that was never checked or controlled. Her parents never set limits for her. They were too involved in their own lives.

Ann, despite her drinking and drugging, managed to finish school and start a brilliant art career only to crash early on in her young life.

Chapter VIII

When I acquired a sponsor she asked me to make a list of twenty-five of my character defects. Twenty-five! Would you believe I could only come up with five? With a little help I found a few more defects of character. The biggest one was my unwillingness to change. I was a creature of habit and although I wasn't drinking I wanted everything else to stay the same.

One of my biggest problems was that I was unable to ask for help. Something in my nature made it impossible to ask another person to do something for me. There were times that I was physically impaired and had to struggle to do simple chores. Instead of asking a neighbor or friend to put out the garbage, I would trudge to the garbage bin and devise some way of getting the bag into the bin. I know that it doesn't seem like much, but now I have learned that people are willing to help. I am still a little reluctant to request help but I do it when I need to.

I am a master of control. I want everything done my way. Yes, I had a lot to learn. Now I know that I must yield to other people. I had to listen to new ideas—even though patience is not one of my virtues. I had been in control for so many years—in business, raising a family, and a caregiver to my parents that control was my middle name. Perhaps, my control was an illusion and it was time for me to sit back and let somebody else do it.

Willingness to change is a major issue and I asked God to help me. I asked God for patience. What is so frightening about changing is that I was finding myself as someone new and wondered how I got that way. I tried to remember myself as that young person before I drank and how I had changed into the hard relentless unlikable person that I had become. Now I was changing again. The program taught me to slow down. Keep it simple and above all, take one day at a time.

As for my religious beliefs they were brought home to me when I visited Thailand. We were taken into a very large Buddhist Temple (but not before removing our shoes). I stood before the golden Buddha and suddenly felt as if I was in the wrong place. Did I have a jealous God? When we were taken to other temples I found that I could not go in. I would approach the door and it was as if a hand was holding me back. I waited patiently outside for my group and meditated on the lovely flowers and trees, watched the people and silently prayed. My mind became clear, refreshed and I was elated.

By admitting that I was an alcoholic, joining AA, starting the Steps, renewing my faith in God—I was on the right path to enlightenment. I really do not have a formal way of praying. Just say what is in my heart. At night, before retiring, I review my day and it has become part of my daily routine. Perhaps, by speaking to another person about my past life it forced me to speak and think more clearly and to really hear their reaction. Saying, "I'm sorry," really had justifications. When I admitted to someone what I had done, a heavy burden was eased even though I felt ashamed and guilty. It wasn't long before I felt as if I could reach out to others. After a few years in the program I felt that I was strong enough to sponsor another person. It was a disaster.

The young woman that approached me was having a terrible time in her marriage. She had stopped drinking but her husband had not. He would not come into the program and he constantly tried to force her to drink. I am not a psychologist and I suggested she and her husband visit a marriage counselor. But, she said, I thought you were my sponsor and could help me. I explained that she was the only one who can make the decision of whether she wanted to keep her marriage and how she was going to do it. I could only suggest the possibilities. I was not a magician. We met a few times and I sensed that her problem was becoming worse. She sent me a lovely plant. The plant withered and died and I took it as an omen: I felt as if I had failed and it was a long time before I was willing to sponsor anyone else.

There are times when I see myself alone on a desert island. I am alone. There is no one else. Who will hear me? It is at those moments when I am closest to finding God.

Imagine being stranded with nothing but sand, sea, and

sky. Survival is my only challenge. I must overcome all obstacles. That is the way I supposed myself to be. In order to leave the desert island I had to firmly admit that I was an alcoholic and take the necessary measures to survive.

At a recent meeting I shared my thoughts about being embarrassed when people told me that they were proud of me. A member, a good friend, told me that I felt the way I did because I had not forgiven myself. I stopped short in my tracks realizing that he was right. I had not forgiven myself. Part of my problem was that I did not think that anyone really forgave me, either. Oh, sure, they mouthed the words, "I'm so proud of you." But, in their heart of hearts, were they really? They were happy I was not drinking and walking the straight and narrow but could my sons really forgive me for causing them pain throughout my drinking career? Could they forgive my divorce? My younger son was the one person most seriously affected. My older son would not accept the fact that I was an alcoholic. He repeatedly said, "Mom, you just like to drink."

Chapter IX

The first time I was asked to tell my story at a meeting I carefully prepared my notes. I had heard other people tell their stories and I thought mine was different. No way! We were all alcoholics and whether we began drinking at the age of 12 or 35 the bottom line was we couldn't safely drink. I told my story but never once resorted to my notes. In my notes I found that I blamed everyone for my problems. After reading them I realized that the fault was mine—mine alone.

Going to rehab was the best thing that I could have done. While I was drinking and my boyfriend was doing drugs, we had never heard about AA or a rehab. Imagine how ignorant we were! I don't remember when it was that we heard about the Betty Ford Institute. I thought it was all for famous people. When I did investigate the program I imagined a place of great luxury. I didn't know that there were other places without the famous names and expense that could achieve the same results. There are some insurance companies that will pay all or some of the costs. Mine did not. However I have a very caring and generous family who loved me enough to insure treatment.

When I started to attend meetings I found that they were

all in churches. Deniably, AA simply did not adhere to the Jewish religion. But, times are changing and I finally have an AA meeting at a reformed synagogue. Not that it matters. All meetings follow the 12 Step program. I was simply angry that we as a people were denying that Jews are not Alcoholics.

There are many issues that can plague the alcoholic. One of them is reporting—that is done in the media. Most recently, it has been reported that drinking alcohol can help avoid heart attacks. It was also reported that it was healthy to drink. (In moderation.) Well, what does that mean to an alcoholic?

To us, it means: No! We do not understand moderation. One drink is too many and a whole bottle is not enough. I suggest that you don't try it. Too many of my fellow travelers have and they lived to regret it.

Many of my friends take medication. They should read the instructions on the bottles carefully. Very often it is written: Not to be taken if you use alcohol.

Very often this advice is ignored and the end result could be a painful death.

Unfortunately, years ago when the doctor ordered a medication for me I would ask if I could drink with the new prescription. When he said no, I wouldn't take the medication. How crazy is that? I ended up with my nerves shattered and being very ill.

One of my close friends is a diabetic. She skips meals so that she can drink. I took the time to visit Alanon. As they suggested, I did drag her to an AA meeting but as they say, "you can lead a horse to water…" I visited her priest and asked if he would speak with her. He did, but that did not help either. My friend insists that she has found God and prays to Him all of the time. Then she is off to have a drink. She will probably go blind or lose a limb or possibly die. Recently, she has been going to a psychiatrist and I believe there may yet be hope for her—I pray that there will be.

If I begin to lose faith I just have to go for a walk and view the beauty of the earth. Somehow, I find serenity and just the sight of a single butterfly can restore a calm attitude.

Many of my friends are agnostics or atheists and we have had many discussions about religion and God. In my case, I exclaim that God is a higher power, a great force of energy. This energy has given me tools to work with. Mainly, a brain, eyes, ears, some talents and it is up to me to put all of those things to work. I do not expect God to do it for me. I think that it is enough that I have received the gifts that I have. The rest is up to me. But, it wasn't always that way. When the pressures of life became too much, I retreated into my cave. And, what and where was that cave?

Me, in a darkened bar, or alone in my room, drinking booze and listening or not, to sad music. It was not beyond me to go to that bar, pick up some other lonely soul and end up in a one-night stand only to wonder the next morning who in the hell that guy was in my bed. In all of the war stories I have heard that was one of the favorite chapters.

I had a job but I also had other occupations. As I have said before, I write and paint, but not in the frenzied way I did when I was drunk. I am happy to say that I have not lost the magic. Now I think that I will never be able to complete all of the projects or develop all of ideas in my mind. I realize that I am very fortunate and I am exceedingly grateful to have come this far with so many blessings. Understanding where I am, how I feel and what I have at hand has made me humble. I know that humility had been one of my character flaws and one downfall of many alcoholics. We get so drunk that we easily forget that we are creatures of the universe and vulnerable to all catastrophes or blessings. When we find a higher power we must remember to be humble and ask for help.

Chapter X

Alcoholics always claim that they have wanderlust. When they are constantly moving from one place to another they romantically claim that it is the gypsy in their soul. Things would fall apart in one place and they would pack up and move to another place where no one would know them, as if a new place would cure them of their alcoholism. Or, perhaps, a career change. In my case I was constantly searching.

I had a great problem being near family and friends who were constantly after me to stop drinking. When the subject arose I would become belligerent and angry. Most of the time, I wished that they would mind their own business. I hated it when they said that Jews don't drink. After our discussions and I would be alone, I would drink more heavily. I was frustrated and angry and would lie to myself about my reasons for drinking, always blaming someone or something else.

Lying becomes a habit with alcoholics. We lie about little things, big things and we lie to make ourselves pure. Alcoholics never want to be outdone. They invent places they have been, movies they have seen, and books they have read. All they really want to do is build their egos because the flip side is so very terrible.

After my divorce and shedding my boyfriend I did meet a wonderful man. Jay was considerate, and probably the kindest person I have ever known. He was too good to be true. The first night he invited me to dinner I was very excited and nervous. I fortified myself with two shots of vodka—or was it three? Whatever! We went to Jay's favorite Italian restaurant and he ordered a bottle of wine. I am sure it was more than acceptable but I tasted the wine and announced that it was vinegary. Naturally, I imagined that I knew the difference. Jay ignored the comment being the gentleman that he was and ordered dinner for us. Thankfully, he didn't suggest some other kind of drink or I would have gotten plastered. Our relationship lasted six months. One drunken night I accused Jay of having an affair with my best friend. In my drunken stupor I wanted to test him. I wanted to hear those wonderful words: I love you. It never happened. I never gave him a chance. I even changed the lock on my door. I knew in my heart that he would never return; in fact, he never called.

My friends asked me what happened and of course I lied. I told everyone that his wife wouldn't give him a divorce and I suggested that we separate. Another big lie. Jay was not married, but I could not think of anything else to say.

Chapter XI

I have never remarried. In fact, I never could maintain a real relationship. I would be involved with a person and then at a certain point I would get drunk and verbally attack my companion to the point of his leaving and never seeing me again.

Most of the time, I would forget what I had said. I can only assume that it was unjustified and very nasty. Usually, I was too embarrassed to pursue the matter. One kindly gentleman suggested I go for help.

When I drank my inner anger surfaced and it didn't matter who became the target. All of the psychological help could not drive out my anger but I believed that my higher power would and could.

Asking for forgiveness allowed me to realize where my anger was coming from. Staying sober allowed me to examine the course of events. I found that I had created my own anger. I could have dealt with my mother and mother-in-law's illnesses differently by explaining my need for emotional support to my husband and seeking professional help. I did neither. I just hated him for not offering, never realizing that he didn't know how to help. I also knew that my stubborn personality insisted on doing everything my way and alone.

As my life became more complicated I thought to do it alone, as it would be harder to explain the procedure to someone else. How wrong I was. I now know that it is impossible to go at it alone and there is nothing wrong in asking for help. AA teaches that concept. I could not have gotten sober alone.

At the meetings that I have attended I have met professional people. Most recently a psychiatrist whose specialty is treating children, an orthopedic surgeon and a heart specialist. All had many years of sobriety but as I listened to their stories I wondered how they could have functioned while they were in their drinking stage. How many patients did they treat while suffering a hangover? The answer is unknown. In the major part of their stories they related that they could not become sober even as they were threatened from being dismissed from their professions, talking to their rabbis or priests, or pressure from their spouses until they themselves asked for help.

When the noted surgeon relayed his story I shuddered to think about the consequences. After many years of drinking the hospital finally dismissed him by telling him he could not practice unless he became sober. He tried but could not stop drinking. One night, as he lay passed out on the kitchen floor his 15-year-old daughter poked him on the back and asked, "Daddy, when are you going to stop drinking?" Her words were like a knife to his heart. The surgeon called Alcoholics Anonymous. The rest is history.

The heart surgeon was not as lucky as the orthopedic

surgeon. When I was drinking I often frequented a certain jazz club where musicians could sit in with the band. Our heart surgeon obviously was a frustrated clarinetist. He played clarinet and drank, drink after drink until he had to be helped off of the stage. I cannot imagine how he would possibly operate the next day while suffering a hangover and undoubtedly shaking hands. Fortunately, for his patients, he was dismissed from the medical profession. I do not know what happened to him, but I can hope that he found the will to become sober.

Chapter XII

Memories are hard to shake and although I adored my father I never thought of him as an alcoholic until I admitted that I was. My father drank every day. In fact, when he woke up in the morning he had a shot of scotch to start the day. By the time he went to bed each night he had finished a bottle of scotch.

My father was a quiet, gentle man. His drinking did not change him, which is very unusual considering statistics. As the first born, with five siblings, a mother who worked to make ends meet and an alcoholic father, he had overwhelming responsibilities. His father was a disillusioned chemist, from Russia, who started his life in the United States by producing hair tonic. When that venture failed he made "bathtub gin". Unfortunately, he drank his own concoction and died at the age of fifty-two from alcoholism.

My grandmother somehow managed to open a furniture store. My father told me stories of how he would drive a horse and wagon to New York City from Yonkers, New York, to buy furniture for the store enduring snowstorms, ice, and a very old, temperamental horse. Whatever story he told it was always with great humor. My father created illusion. He wanted everyone to be happy and all stories to have a happy ending.

My family was all secular Jews. There is no evidence of religious adherence except for the celebration of holidays. I am not sure where or how my father became religious. Every morning he would don his prayer shawl and tefilm (leather straps that wind around the arm for Morning Prayer) and chant Hebrew prayers. I once asked him why he did that. He responded by saying that he was thanking God for the day that had been and praying that the days to come would be good. He performed that ritual every day of his life from the age of thirteen. While recalling my father's religious devotion I go back to my childhood. Our synagogue was a warm and comforting place. The housing for the Torah was surrounded by frescos of animals and fauna. The dais was shining brass and red carpeting. The aroma was oak and cedar. Women sat in the balcony behind a lace curtain and the men sat downstairs, true to orthodox traditions.

As a young female child I could sit with my father because I had not yet started to menstruate. I would sit between my uncle and my father. They smelled of cologne and rich tobacco. I did not understand any of the praying but I did understand the warmth, love and the feeling of being secure. I never experienced that special feeling again.

My father was an auctioneer. The profession suited him. It was the days of the Great Depression and we suffered like everybody else economically. The difference was we didn't know we were poor. Once my father bought a toy store to be auctioned and I had every doll and accessories that a little girl could possibly want. Another store he bought was a grocery store that had had a fire and all of the labels had been washed from the cans. Every night we would guess what was in the can. Usually, it was beets or fruit cocktail.

The last thing he bought was a hotel in Florida. My mother, father, aunt and uncle were on their way to vacation and I received a call from him. He told me to pack up the children and meet them in Mt. Dora; a place I had never heard of. It seems that a man showed my uncle a brochure of a hotel he wanted to sell and my uncle and father bought the hotel without seeing it while flying to Miami. It is hard to imagine that they were sober while doing it.

I did pack up my kids and travel to Florida to help them. I was very devoted to my family. My husband stayed at home. (It was Tax Season.) And, what a hotel! 99 rooms, golf course, Olympic swimming pool—the works! However, we were understaffed not to mention that we were very new to the business. My father said that he could learn the hotel business in 3 days: someone will tell me what I do wrong and someone else tell me what I should do and I'll know the hotel business. Fantasy land!

My mother baby-sat the kids while I became the chambermaid, caterer, baker, and person in charge of personnel. It was in the days before Civil Rights and black people could not sleep on the premises. When the dishwasher quit I went to the local jail and hired whatever criminal they had on hand. We had thirty people staying at the hotel and I prepared breakfast. I was all of thirty-one years old. However, I had good training. My mother was a taskmaster and I was well schooled in cleaning, cooking, and whatever since I had always been expected to help as my mother worked with my father. I think it is called survival.

The other thing that was wrong was that my father had suffered a few heart attacks and was on a medication called "Comidan". Comidan was a new drug at the time and the doctor never mentioned that it should not be taken with alcohol. The doctor had no clue that my father was an alcoholic. At first, my father had double vision. I took him to a doctor in Florida who told him not to drink and return to New York and go to the hospital. No, we had to have a happy ending. Right? My father would not conceive of himself being a burden. Back at the hotel my father told me he was going to have a nap. Went to his room and drank a bottle of Four Star Hennessy—and died! He was 59 years old.

That left me with a body to bring back to New York, an inconsolable mother, three small children (if you count my husband) and a hotel. We closed the hotel and later sold it.

Soon after, I suffered a bout of depression. I desperately missed my father. I had no support system. I could easily identify with him by doing the thing he liked best. Drink! And so it began.

Chapter XIII

I have said before that alcoholics lie. I was a champion liar. I lied my way into jobs. I lied about my education. I lied to make people happy. I lied about my drinking habits. I embellished upon my children's achievements. Lying was my major bad characteristic. A basic problem is that I have a huge imagination. Unfortunately, I could never seem to get my priorities right. It never dawned on me that I could have gotten the job without lying. After I was hired I always worked hard and was able to achieve success. When other designers were being fired I always received raises and congratulations on a job well done. I must have been doing something right.

When my mother became ill and my mother-in-law became more dependent upon me, I decided that I would lose my mind if I had to stay at home with them. In order to supplement our income I freelanced at jobs. I designed handkerchiefs for a company in Madeira. I had seen an ad in the *Times*, submitted samples, and was hired immediately. I also sold drawings of stuffed animals to manufactures by filling my portfolio with drawings and canvassing the Toy Center in New York.

At that time I had a small home business. I held after

school art classes. A small group of children would attend and together we explored the wonderful world of art. I was untrained but that didn't bother me. I never gave it a thought.

Over the years I had taught myself to paint in various mediums: sculpt, wood carve and print. I did it by reading books and following procedures. I exhibited my work in art shows and became a member of the Sculptor's Society of New York. For a period of time I enjoyed the possibilities of primitive art. Going to the lumberyard I would buy pine boards, sketch my subject, carve in bas-relief, colorfully paint the figure and prepare it for hanging. Twice a year I exhibited in Greenwich Village, at the famous art fair, on the sidewalk, with other artists. I carved and painted 289 pieces during that time, sold all and bought myself a dishwasher and a mink coat.

I gave up the business to get out of house. Returned to school and took a pattern making course. I had decided to become a fashion designer and get a full time job.

Completing the course, I was ready and elected to be a children's wear designer. An ad appeared in *Women's Wear Daily* that suited me and I applied. When asked what my previous experience was—I made up 3 fictitious names. The man that interviewed me was very impressed. I, of course, wondered how, since the companies did not exist.

At the time, I didn't know that I didn't need to know pattern making, sewing or cutting. All I had to do was draw a picture, hand it to a pattern maker who gave it to a cutter, who gave it a sample hand, who sewed the sample. I chose the buttons and bows. The salesmen who sold fabrics and accessories were very quick show me the latest samples and using them they would receive large orders. I became a very popular designer with the working crowd. I was very popular at home as well. I was a machine that managed the house, laundry, meals, kids, husband, and animals and kept everyone happy—except myself. I can't imagine what miracle I thought would come along to change things. Escape was easy. I dove right into the bottle.

During the years I worked I produced more than 10,000 original designs. Every year we were responsible for five seasons: winter, spring, summer, fall and holiday. I worked for eight years and then my world blew up—of my own doing.

Alcoholic, divorced, cruising in the fast lane, jet setting, and searching. One night at a penthouse party where the booze flowed and the candy dishes were filled with cocaine, a certain kind of revelation was revealed to me. We were all fifty-year-old hippies and the scene was definitely not what I wanted. True to the alcoholic in me, I moved. Of course, I thought starting in a new place, a new life was going to change things. Are you laughing, yet?

Encouraged by my son I moved to Israel. It would have been fine if I had located in Tel Aviv and found a job, but no, I needed adventure. I did start in Tel Aviv but only for three days. During that time I heard about a village in the north of Israel, Maalot. The Jewish Agency wanted an art colony in the north of Israel in order to attract more tourists to the area.

I boarded the train from Tel Aviv to Natanya, a charming city on the Mediterranean. There seemed to be no seats available on the train, except for one.

Of course, I didn't speak Hebrew but that didn't bother me. I asked the young man next to the empty seat if the seat was taken, hoping he spoke English. "No, I was saving it for you," he replied in the King's English. As coincidence would have it, he was a sculptor on his way to Maalot. Malcolm and I were to become the beginning of the anticipated art colony.

Maalot is ten kilometers from Lebanon, located on a hilltop in northern Israel amidst pine forests, with a spectacular view of towns, villages and the sea. The air is clean and the light ideal for an artist. I had no trouble imagining myself living there.

After meeting the other artists with the same objective I immediately signed up for the project. I had to return to the States, resolve my affairs, quit my job, and pack my furniture and belongings that would later be shipped to Israel when I was situated in my own apartment.

It was January of 1977. I returned home and hurriedly packed. I packed photo albums, dishes, pots and pans, linens, anything that I thought I would need. I think I packed the garbage. During all of the packing I managed to tape my record albums, dance around and drink.

With me everything had to be a party.

One night my doorbell rang about midnight. It was one of my boyfriends. It was January and snowing. He stood at my door in his shirt sleeves. First, he asked me for money to pay the cab driver, and then he rushed into the house. He told me that he had been to Las Vegas and had lost a lot of money and then borrowed more from a bookie. Now the bookie was after him and was going to break his legs—or worse. I couldn't help him but either the bookie or the booze would get him and he would die either way. A truck was coming the next morning to take my cartons and furniture and I was leaving. I left him to figure it out for himself.

Chapter XIV

People, cities, countries have encountered problems with alcohol. Back in the 1600's gin was becoming the ruination of England. Gin was considered "Mother's Ruin", in more ways than one. In the United States prohibition was introduced and more problems were created. More than if we had ignored the entire alcohol situation. Gangsters had a heyday. Bootlegging became a big business. "Bathtub gin" became the ruination of many families, as it did in my family.

My grandfather had a small factory manufacturing hair tonic that required alcohol in its production. Local hoodlums held my grandfather at gunpoint and acquired the factory. As a last resort, grandfather went into the business of producing his own brand of vodka. He fermented potato peels and with his own formula created a marketable product. His sister's husband became his distributor. For the first time in his life he was finally making money. Unfortunately, he drank his own product. I have mentioned this before but it is a point I can refer to casually.

While tracing my family tree of alcoholic members I am sure it did not begin with my grandfather. His father owned an inn in Russia—the last station before Siberia.

My grandfather worked with his parents until he was sent to Moscow to study chemistry. It was unusual for a Jew to attend the university and I assume the family had enough money to pay for the tuition. Upon graduation Grandfather was destined for the Russian army. His brothers and sisters preceded him to the States and were waiting for him. The story is short and sweet. He made his way to the United States determined not to become a soldier. I don't know anything about his journey but recently we found his Ellis Island entry permit and his American citizen papers. Intelligent, ambitious, qualified to become an outstanding person and now the big "What if...?" he wasn't an alcoholic. We will never know.

As science advances we are knowledgeable about DNA. The fine threads of genes that are passed from generation to generation. Am I to believe that I inherited alcoholism from that ancestor who was an alcoholic? That would probably take me back to Lot and Noah. There are many records describing the use of wine in the lives of ancient people.

After the destruction of Sodom the two daughters of Lot believed that they were the only three people left on earth. They deemed it their duty to preserve mankind.

They plied their father with wine, had sex with him and both daughters gave birth to sons. (Genesis Chapter19:31) Obviously, these ancient people had grape vines and the knowledge of not only knowing how to produce wine but of what the after effects were.

As for Noah, he was knowledgeable in agriculture, mathematics, architecture, and survival tactics.

In Genesis Chapter 9:19 the Bible describes Noah planting a vineyard and the results of his drunkenness. Throughout the Bible wine is referred to as a major aphrodisiac. If the scientists are correct in the theory that we inherit our forefather's genes, I wonder how many of us have carried the gene of alcoholic illness.

In all of our religions wine plays a major part in our rites and ceremonies. When I was young no one thought of substituting grape juice for the wine at the Passover Seder for the little kids. We followed the service, drank the wine, got wild and eventually went to sleep. My cousins and I all looked forward to the Seder. We were born alcoholics.

I assume that since we were born into the Jewish religion we are all descendants of Lot, Noah, Abraham, Sarah, Leah and Jacob. DNA testing has shown that the Jewish people have inherited the genes of our ancestors. Through careful study we know that the men of Sephardic heritage all have similar DNA inherited from their mothers. Their mothers inherited their genes from their fathers. There is a law in Israel that states that if the mother is Jewish so are her children. Before DNA was available I never understood the law. Actually, this was a hand down from Moses. I am constantly astounded to learn how clever the ancient people were. Recently, while reading the Bible I came across a passage that totally bewildered me and set

68

me thinking. In Genesis Chapter 5:4 it is written that Adam lived a hundred and thirty years, and begat a son in his own likeness, after his image (Seth). Did Adam clone Seth?

The history of the Bible is 5,763 years old, according to the Jewish calendar. Each year we read the Torah (Bible) in September beginning with Genesis and somewhere around April we have reached the giving of the Ten Commandments. The Tenth Commandment tells us not to envy anybody and to apply reason through thought, speech and deed.

In Jewish tradition controlling one's actions is the simplest level of self-control and observance. By giving this commandment God is telling us that, yes, we can control our very thoughts and direct them for good purposes. We are given the gift of human intelligence in order to be able to sift out the good from the bad. The Torah often refers to physical realities and drives of everyday life. Very often it gets in the way of spiritual growth. The body and what it represents becomes an adversary to the soul.

In such conditions the body is struggling under the weight of what is expected of us and its requirements. Finding a higher power helps us refine and transform the body and mind. If we are unable to find a higher power we can easily collapse under the load.

A higher power will help elevate us to a higher level. We will be encouraged to take the physical body away from damning situations.

While searching for our higher power the chances are that we will be caught in a period of reflection. The mirror of our souls. We ask ourselves, "Did I really do that?"

Some of the memories can shake us to the heights of disgust and down to the pits of regret.

Recently, I came in contact with a friend that I hadn't seen for a long time. We agreed to meet for lunch. During that time I confessed that I had been to rehab and hadn't had a drink for many years. She was delighted, congratulated me and said that she had known I was an alcoholic and now regretted that she hadn't said anything to me about changing. She also said that during that time I was "wild". I didn't think it affected me but I suddenly lost my appetite and ended by pushing the food around on my plate.

Afterwards, I played with what she had said: "I was wild!" Well, if I was so wild and she had such a dislike for what I was doing, why did she hang around? The only answer I could come up with was that at the time she needed me. I was a party girl and she was a mouse. I would not let her remark put me down. I needed to confirm my self-confidence. I knew that I had become a better person and she was still a mouse.

Staying sober is self-control of the highest level. When I drank I had no self-control. In recovery I have found that there are those lazy days when I do not want to attend a meeting but I know that I must, especially, when I am under pressure, or nervous, or just having a mood swing. Reaching for a drink would be so very easy.

Chapter XV

I have never been able to keep a diary. On the other hand, what would I have written? Would I have been honest? Probably, not. Oh, yes, I would have recorded the events of trips, holidays, birthdays, and all of things that people write in diaries. But would I have told about the one-night stands or the blackouts? Is it better to keep some secrets locked into the bad memory corner of our minds? I have shared some of my dark secrets with my sponsor, but I am sure many details have been lost.

What is the point, you might ask. I have found by relating about where I have been and what I have done has been a way of cleansing my soul. I have been able to dispense with the burden of guilt. There are a few items that still cling and there is a chance I will never be able to dispense with them.

It is interesting that as a child I readily accepted God and continued to do so well into adulthood. My first pregnancy was a disaster. In my seventh month I began to bleed. My doctor determined that the fetus died and requested that I have a legal abortion by a panel of doctors. I was required to have rabbit tests performed in order to determine if the pregnancy was valid. All the tests came back positive. I was denied an abortion. My mother became hysterical believing that I would be poisoned by the dead fetus. My doctor told me do a lot of exercise, run, jump, etc. I wore myself out, day after day, trying to induce labor. I had God in my mind and I accepted my fate.

I remember reading a book by Fulton Osler that helped me to interpret the Bible. I fortunately found the inner peace I had been seeking.

When labor pains finally started I was prepared for the worst. I was the only patient in the labor room. On or about midnight, I felt the violent urge to void. Frantically, I rang for a nurse but no one came. Somehow, I retrieved a bedpan and sitting on it, gave birth to a mummified fetus. I stared at it for a long time but could not determine the sex. I was young, inexperienced but not afraid. I covered the remains with a towel and slid it under the bed. For the remainder of the night I lay awake talking to God and thanking Him for taking a child that was not suppose to be. It was God's will and I accepted His will.

Tests later showed that although the fetus had died the afterbirth remained alive and all of the testing returned positive. Curettage was performed and I had to be tested for three months to be sure everything had been removed. (Poor rabbits; they die after the tests are done.)

I wanted a child and I trusted God. It wasn't long before I became pregnant again. Well into my sixth month I had not felt life and wondered if I was going to go through the same ordeal. It was January and my husband and I were attending a rehearsal by the Philharmonic Orchestra with Toscanini conducting. We entered the hall and took our seats in the first row. Toscanini raised his baton and with the first chords of Beethoven's Fifth, my baby moved and I yelled, "Oh!" Toscanini stopped the orchestra, turned to see who had interrupted him, looked at me holding my stomach, smiled, blew me a kiss and said, "Madonna." He turned and resumed conducting. In March, my healthy son was born. My child was in my arms and God was in my heart.

I know that I have always walked with God and talked with God. In desperation, there have been times when I have asked, "Why?" In AA, we are told that God does not give you more than you can handle. Then I ask, "How much can I handle?" Looking for answers I returned to the Bible and my thoughts and readings were directed to Abraham. Why I was directed and how, remains the mystery.

Abraham is regarded as the father of three religions: Judaism, Christianity, and Muslim. We are all children of Abraham, we must answer to God's call. We must start a new journey and become a stranger in a strange land. We must give up what we have so desperately clung to. By giving up our addictions we face the land of reality and we become strangers that are able to rebuild a new life.

Legend has it that Terah, Abraham's father, and his sons lived beyond the Euphrates and served other gods. God led Abraham beyond the River and led him through all the land of Canaan. Somehow he knew that worshiping other gods was wrong. When Abraham confronts his father with his knowledge his father replies, "I know that there is only one God and worshiping idols is wrong, but what shall I do with the other people who have ordered me to serve before them?"

Abraham enters his father's shop where the idols are created he and smashes them. King Nimrod orders Abraham to be burnt in a furnace. Miraculously he survives. Other legends describe Abraham moving to Phoenicia to teach astronomy and other sciences to Egyptians, who passed them on to the Greeks. Story after story, legend after legend. All of the stories were equally fascinating. However, we finally accept the one story as written in the Bible.

God calls to Abraham and he answers, "I am here." (The same answer that Moses gave when he ascended Mount Sinai—in Hebrew: enainu.) The lord commands Abram, as he was called at the time, to leave his home and seek the Promised Land where He will make of Abram a leader of people, a great nation, and renames him, Abraham, and although Abraham is now seventy-five years old declares that he will have a son. We go on to great adventure. Sarah's handmaiden, Hagar, mates with Abraham and gives birth to Ishmael. Sarah after being visited by angels gives birth to Isaac. No matter how many times I read the stories, I become caught up in the power.

Reading biblical history can sometimes be very

confusing but the parables are great. From Abraham's story I derived that I, too, had to change my life. I had to become a stranger to the life I was leading. I had to reconstruct and build a new life without my alcoholic friends and my bad habit of relying on alcohol.

Many people in the stories from the Bible describe starting anew. Abraham, Jesus, Hagar, Moses, to name a few. All the mentioned people willingly, entered the desert. There is only one thing more deadly than the silence of the desert and that is a blackout. The horror of not being able to remember where you have been or what you have done.

When I was forty-eight I actually was crazy enough to backpack it alone in Europe. The world wasn't so crazy then. (Only me.)

I remember very little of the trip except that I never traveled before and I was very envious of the kids that were out there living their lives. I remember Paris vividly, especially, the bathroom. It had a bidet and a bathtub bigger than my bed. I tried to be a well-behaved tourist in Paris and only drank in my room after dinner to be sure I wouldn't get blazing drunk and tell the Frenchmen what I thought of them.

London was different. I loved the pubs. My kind of a place! One day I did visit the Jewish section and enjoyed some ethnic food. But this is all digressing. Back to Israel.

Once, while visiting friends in Israel who farmed in the desert region known as the "Arriva", I assembled my paints and canvas and drove to the sand colored hills of the Negev. The silence was almost unbearable. I constantly looked over my shoulder sure that someone was watching me. I had my dog with me and I knew that he would signal should anybody approach. I was alone but wary. I was afraid of the silence. On a distant hill I could see a mountain goat grazing.

I returned from my outing with a canvass that expresses the loneliness and desperation that I had felt. When my friend saw the canvass he was overwhelmed by the colors and said that he knew the place, but asked me how I dared to enter the area. He went on to say that the area had been laid with mines and that there were signs there that said not to enter. I stared at him, dumbfounded. I did not recall seeing one sign that said: Danger. Had I truly walked with God?

I am not afraid of the silence anymore. I welcome it. During my silent times I am able to meditate, evaluate my day, and communicate with my higher power. I believe that God has provided me with guidance and is directing my life with His every day miracles. I just have to look into the eyes of my children and grandchildren to know that I have received the miracle of God's blessings

Chapter XVI

It would be impossible to write this story without telling about my cousin Carla. Whenever, I recall my drinking days my thoughts revert to Carla and her tragic story. I only write it to help other young people who think they are living the high life and cannot see into the future and see themselves as helpless addicts.

My cousin gave birth to Carla at the age of 43, her father 50. Carla, the product of a second marriage. Her siblings were 18 and 16. From birth Carla was the spoiled darling of a very wealthy and indulging family. Expensive clothes, exotic vacations, lavish home styles, foreign cars, were the norm for the family. Nothing was denied Carla. Carla was beautiful, talented, bright, and wild. I don't think she ever heard the word, "no." By the age of 15 she was a wild, undisciplined teenager with bad habits and obscene language. After being expelled from high school for the use of drugs and bad mouthing the principal her family punished her by taking her to Acapulco, Mexico, and then bought her a new car when she promised to reform.

When the problem became worse she was shuttled off to a psychologist who suggested that the entire family should receive counseling. My cousin, Carla's mother, was and is an alcoholic. Her father, a diamond in the rough, succeeded in life by his own wit and bravado. His use of street language was extremely colorful and Carla had a vocabulary of all the choice words. I would say that the family was completely dysfunctional.

I had a close relationship with my cousins and would visit often. It was painful to see Carla wasting her young life. She did not return to school and often stayed in bed until midafternoon when her social life would start. Hopping into her convertible she would head to the nearest drug spot only to return home in the wee hours of the morning drunk and drugged out.

I remember one night when she offered me to accompany her. They lived in Westchester, N.Y., and we drove to the East Bronx where she picked up her stash of drugs. I was furious that she had taken me to a very dangerous section of New York. When I confronted her she said that the only reason she had invited me to go along was that she didn't want to go there alone. I immediately told her parents and her father went into a wild rage. Carla turned to him and told him to drop dead. I, in turn, whipped around and smacked her face. The next morning she apologized to me. Carla wanted to be stopped and recognized me as a force.

One day I received a frantic phone call from my cousin. Carla had totaled her car and was in jail. The young man riding with her was in the hospital. Carla had been drunk and crashed into a train abutment. Now, no car and her first DUI. The judge ordered Carla to attend AA but she never did and she was arrested on charges of not following the judge's orders. She was ordered to a rehab. My cousins sent Carla to a dude ranch in Arizona for rehabilitation. When she returned home they bought her a new car. Shortly after, her mother received a phone call in the middle of the night. Carla had been found lying naked and passed out on a deserted street in the Bronx.

The result was a concussion, broken collarbone, two black eyes, and pneumonia. Of course, she had made a bad drug deal and her car was taken and she was badly beaten.

Six weeks later she was on the street again. She was forbidden to drive but she would take the keys to her mother's car and storm and rage out of the house. I begged my cousin to call the police and turn Carla in as a drug addict. I explained tough love to her, but my cousin would hear none of it.

Carla resumed her exploits and within three years had three abortions. Now she was eighteen. She left home and took refuge with a seventy-five-year-old man who became her pimp. On occasion Carla would visit her mother but only to ask for money and food. It was a heartbreaking situation.

I had moved to Israel and in desperation my cousin called me and asked if Carla could come to Israel and stay with me. I agreed but only if Carla would do as I asked her. I made arrangements for Carla to volunteer on a kibbutz.

The result was a perfect miracle or could have been. The people on the kibbutz were thrilled with Carla. She was alcohol and drug free, she was a very hard worker, and was actually attending classes to learn Hebrew. I had such high hopes! Not to be. My cousin kept writing letters to Carla telling her how much she missed her and relating all the news about the parties and places they had gone to and restaurants they had eaten in. Her mother's letters drove Carla crazy, crazy enough to want to go back to the States.

Life on a kibbutz is the flip side of a coin of life in the United States. Most of your time is spent wearing work clothes and dedicating your day to work. Carla first worked in the community dining room cleaning tables. Later she was assigned to the kitchen helping to cook. She was asked if she would like to work in the kibbutz factory inspecting the finished product, which was furniture.

She agreed and really liked doing the work, amazing as it may seem.

We next find Carla with a boyfriend and they want to get married. The young man is from Peru and doesn't speak much English. But, yes, they want to get married. Actually, everything is set for the wedding except the young man hightails it back to Peru and Carla is left standing at the altar and pregnant.

She returns to America and has the baby, shortly afterward leaves her child with her mother and older sister to raise. By this time, my cousin has moved to Florida and convinces Carla to join them. Everything possible is done to make a new life for Carla and for a while things are going well until one day as she is crossing the street—drinking a beer—she is hit by a car and killed.

Carla's story is only one of many. The thing that makes it unusual is that Carla was the daughter of a Jewish family that had everything. Can we blame the "Carlas" on the sudden explosion of the drug scene or having enough money to buy drugs and alcohol? Is it the exposure to the glamour of television and movies and the desire to be glamorous? I believe Carla's downfall was having a dysfunctional family. An alcoholic mother and overly doting father who both lived in their tree houses.

Whenever I go to an AA meeting and listen to the stories of the beautiful young women that I see there, I remember Carla. I want to tell them Carla's story.

Chapter XVII

When I first started attending AA meetings there were very few women. Gradually, over the years, more and more women started coming through the door. Now, it seems, there are an equal number of men and women at the meetings. I wonder what has happened. Are we coming out of the closest? I guess so!

This is a question really worth examining. In the AA *Big Book* most of the stories relate to men. There are very few stories about drunken women. Surely, there have always been alcoholic women in every society. It is only in the past twenty years, or so, that women have really been frequenting bars. In the older bars, or saloons, there was always a separate door that said: "Ladies' Entrance." I presume that the ladies that entered did not fraternize with the gentlemen in the saloon. But rather sipped their sherry quietly with the other ladies. After prohibition all of that changed. Women smoked in public, hung off of the same bar stools as the men and belted back their booze with not such ladylike mannerisms.

Certainly the ladies on television shows, when meeting for lunch, first order a glass of wine or something harder.

How about Thelma and Louise knocking back a few beers in a saloon one gloomy night? All acceptable situations now. The ladies have stepped out of their living rooms into society and now they have come to AA for help.

Many of the rehab centers have recognized the changes and every day new books and pamphlets are published especially for women alcoholics. The word is out!

Recent studies have shown that girls are more vulnerable than boys to the use of tobacco, alcohol and drugs. I don't know who conducted the studies but I don't believe it. As in ethnic, religious, or gender groups we all have our problems. Boys as well as girls crave being popular with one another and the opposite sex, and sometime will go to any length to achieve it. I know that girls will resort to make-up, and try to wear the leading fashion but it is probably to impress their female friends.

There was a time that girls were ashamed of their developing breasts and developed poor posture in trying to hide the fact. Not any more. Cleavage seems to be the thing as we see by watching television and the movies. Girls and boys are smoking and some cannot wait until they reach legal drinking age. That doesn't mean that they are not able to obtain alcohol, mostly beer, before they are of age. I have seen girls at parties and Bat and Bar Mitzvah's dressed like movie stars, way beyond their age. They seem more sophisticated than their mothers. How does a parent of a thirteen-year-old girl allow her to appear as a "tramp"?

***

At an affair, not too long ago, while in the ladies' room, a young girl standing next to me at the mirror searched in her bag for a lipstick and a condom slipped out of her bag. She was totally unfazed. I was stunned. I knew she had been drinking from the odor of alcohol stemming from her. I couldn't help wondering who was taking her home and how far she would go. I wanted to sit her down and have a long talk with her, but I wasn't her mother or a close relative and I didn't think she would want to hear what I had to say, anyway.

It wasn't too long ago that I told my older granddaughter that I was a virgin when I got married, as were most of my generation. She looked at me in great wonder. I wasn't brave enough to ask her what her experiences were. I suppose I am like that ostrich burying my head in the sand. Of course, when I was drinking I was not exactly a "goody-goody." I wish I were brave enough to tell her about some of my exploits and how I almost was led to ruin. All she sees now is a little gray-haired grandmother who makes chicken soup and tells stories about her dinosaur days.

I do have great faith in the present generation. I know that they will survive as we did. However, their parents are supposedly more aware, certainly more than mine were, and I hope more decorum and spiritually can be forth coming.

Years ago a popular television would ask, "It's ten

o'clock, do you know where your children are?"

I wonder how many parents can answer that question now. I see the teenagers in malls, at theaters, driving cars—without an adult. Some of them are able to beam into home with the use of their cell phones. Some don't bother. Recently, I heard about a sweet sixteen party where the mother had rented two hotel rooms. One room was for food, the other, for dancing. Unfortunately, there was no adult in attendance. The result was a riot and the police had to be summoned.

Drugs and alcohol were found. Surprise! If this is the climate of sixteen-year-olds, what are they going to be when they reach college, if they reach college?

I try to look back at my teenage years and I was adventurous, but I would have died first rather than embarrass my family by having my father have to get me out of jail. Unfortunately, I did not carry that attitude about embarrassing my family when I started drinking. I look at the kids and think, there by the grace of God, there go I.

Chapter XVIII

When I was three years into recovery my daughter-in-law uttered an idle thought: "I'd love to have Sara's Bat Mitzvah in Israel." That utterance grew from a small idea into reality and a major experience in my life.

One year after the initial planning, fifteen of our immediate family was seated on a plane heading for Israel. Myself, my two sons, their wives and children, my former husband, and my daughter-in-law's parents. The eldest person being seventy-nine and the youngest, two and half.

During the six-day war, Israeli troops crossed into Jordan and reclaimed all of Jerusalem. Thirty years ago my husband and I had stayed at the Inter-Continental Hotel that Jordan had built on the desecrated Hebrew Cemetery. I was unaware that as a Jew I should not be staying at that hotel. On a moonlit night I stood on my balcony overlooking the Holy City and watched the sun come up. I could hear the tinkle of bells as a goat herder passed below and the call to prayer from the Mosque. As the day progressed we visited East Jerusalem to be amused by the tourists riding on the sorry-looking camels.

Now, thirty years later, I am in Jerusalem with my

children and grandchildren watching the same sorry-looking camels, only this time I am staying at the King David Hotel. We have all come to Israel not only for my granddaughter's Bat Mitzvah but for my daughter-in-law, for her mother, and my Bat Mitzvah. As adult women we had never had the welcoming ceremony into womanhood as the boys had into manhood. In our time, women were barely acknowledged. How times have changed. Not only were we going to make up for lost time, but we would be Bar Mitzvahed on the recently unearthed southern steps of the original temple, located on the reverse side of the Western Wall, facing David's City. Above us loomed the massive Golden Dome of Haram-as-Sharif. Its shadow reminded me that we were standing on the steps of the original temple. A shiver went through my body and I was truly humbled.

We would each be required to read a passage from the sacred book of the Torah. It had taken me three months to study and memorize my portion in Hebrew. We were all prepared.

My granddaughter, Sara, was first. Unself-conscious and confident she stepped up on the podium to meet the rabbi and face the Torah. Her face lit up into a beautiful smile and she took command. At that moment she represented all of the women in our families that had come before her. I prayed that she would continue to achieve, and live up to all of her potential and become a leader of her people.

How proud I was and yet so humble at being able to

receive this great gift from God.

We continued our trip throughout Israel. At every site we visited I experienced a feeling of spirituality. It seemed so remarkable that we were actually walking on the same paths, following in the footsteps of the ancient people of the Bible. I found myself talking to God, again. Not everyone is fortunate enough to visit Israel, but we all can read the Bible and live the stories in our own minds.

Our trip included a tour of Jordan and the ancient ruins of Petra. At Jordan's border we had to wait for a Jordanian guide. Our Israeli guide and driver were not allowed into Jordan. When the new guide handed me a visa, I burst into tears. No, not tears. I began crying hysterically. The kind man patted my back and kept saying, "Don't cry, mama." I explained that I had lived in Israel and after so many years of not having peace with Jordan I was suddenly able to visit their country and be accepted as a friend.

I told him that Israel and Jordan would know peace and that no mother would cry again over a son being wounded or killed in a war. While drying my tears I felt the great presence of God and wondered if I was glowing with a special aura. As we drove the miles to Petra I sat in stunned silence.

Petra is a city in the desert of Jordan. It is situated around the famous carved ruins of what has become a world attraction. Four thousand years before Christ, the trail in the desert was used as a route by traders that linked China,

India and Southern Arabia with wealthy goods from the Mediterranean markets of Greece, Egypt and Syria. The area is rich in archeological remnants of Stone Age, early settlers, and the Edomite people who are mentioned in the Bible. Petra, the rose and red clay remains, were carved out of the sandstone by the Nabataen Arabs. Most of the edifices are four or five stories tall. The remains of what once were a monastery, a temple and a treasury building. Remember that they did not have modern tools and probably with the use of ropes and chisels they had to work long diligent hours to create the buildings. They are literally carved out of the rock. What remains now is a legacy of the hands of God and nature.

We road on horseback from the city of Petra to the ruins, and were able to enter the buildings and hike around the surrounding area. Our guide pointed to a hilltop where we could see a shrine that had been erected. He said that Aaron, the brother of Moses, was buried there. I found that fact fascinating. When I returned home I went to the Bible and after an extensive search found that Aaron had been buried somewhere in northern Lebanon. Well, it made for a good story—at the time—and perhaps it is true, certainly logical because it was the area where the Jewish people wandered for forty years.

Touring Israel will induce spirituality. It doesn't matter if one is Christian, Jewish or Moslem, somehow when you are told that you are walking in the footsteps of Christ, it has to penetrate one's soul.

We returned home and each of us had our special

memories stored in our photo albums, our stories, our heads and our hearts. I am grateful that I was sober. It never would have happened if I were still drinking.

Chapter XIX

The years pass and sobriety becomes a way of life. As we age and our friends begin to have health problems. Some of our friends die. This is one of the dilemmas of life. When this happens having faith in God or a higher power is best thing that can happen to us. Without faith we could easily slip into depression and chaos. Our lives could become unmanageable.

As a recovering alcoholic I know that I must not get too thirsty, hungry or tired. I don't skip a meal if I can help it and I drink plenty of water, sodas and coffee. I take my medications and vitamins as directed and follow an exercise regime. Now that I am older I find that I need a nap in the afternoon to refresh me. I don't see my old friends anymore because many have moved or died. New friends are hard to come by. If I feel that I need company I visit with my children or bravely attend the nearby senior center. However, that can be depressing or, maybe, it is just my attitude.

I cannot help but think that I learn many things from my dog. He has enduring patience and undying trust in me. Does he question me? Perhaps, he does and shows it when he tugs on his leash and doesn't want to go the way I want to go. I have to have the same faith in God. Of course, I question God or I wouldn't be a thinking person, but there is nothing I can do about the events that take place.

I question the Holocaust and the killing of six thousand Jewish people. I question man's inhumanity to man. I question 9/11 and the killing of innocent people in the Twin Towers. I can wait for answers but I know that there will be none forth coming. All I can do is have undying faith for without believing in my higher power, I will have nothing.

There are times when I delve into the prospect of being reincarnated. In what form would I return to earth? Would I be punished for the sins I committed in my former lives? If I returned in a human form and knew what my life had been, how would I change things?

Reincarnation states that the spirit comes to the earth many times. It seems a wonderful, divine plan, which offers an opportunity to expand in our awareness and correct that which needs to be corrected. This belief is widely accepted among most religions of the East. In the West most churches deny the doctrines of reincarnation. Recent polls regarding the subject indicate that the majority of Americans do believe in reincarnation. Obviously, this is a very personal matter. Faith, perhaps nurtures the idea that the spirit will endure while still on earth.

I think of having become sober as having become reincarnated. That the person I was had died and a new person evolved. In considering reincarnation, we are dealing with the aspect of the spirit. Certainly, I appeared the same, had the same talents, the same family, and the same opinions. But I was sober. I could deal with the past by not struggling with the same problems and circumstances. I was seeking to attain a clearer understanding of myself and of God and with each other. What is more important—I was moving onward.

Chapter XX

The cause of alcoholism appears to be a blend of genetic, physical, psychological, environmental and social factors. The risk of a person becoming an alcoholic is more likely if their parent suffered from the disease of alcoholism. Alcoholism has a higher rate among young people and the elderly, usually because the symptoms are not easily recognized until the affected person becomes alcohol dependent.

The alcoholic's craving for alcohol makes abstinence extremely difficult. Denial is almost the outstanding reason why abusers continue to drink. The goal of treatment is abstinence. It is not easy to abstain when the drink is right under your nose.

Now that I am retired I do attend more social functions with seniors where alcoholic drinks are in abundance. It has become easier for me to stay with my soft drink since a bottle of medication that I have has been clearly marked: "Do not take alcohol with this medication."

I am quite sure that 99% of the people in the room have a similar medication, yet most of them are drinking booze.

Actually, most of them know the consequences but for now they are living in the moment. At a recent Bar

Mitzvah celebration, my cousin threw all care to the wind and after consuming one two many fell and broke her hip. Drink for seniors are lethal. The older we get the less tolerance we have for alcohol without realizing it. Our blood pressure may be too high or we might have osteoporosis, not to mention heart disease. Consuming alcohol can only put us at risk for dangerous falls or heart attacks.

Certainly, there are enough magazine and newspaper articles informing us as to the many possibilities of disaster caused by drinking.

The condominium community I live in has its fair share of seniors and we do have parties. The majority drink the wrong drinks and eat the wrong food. For some reason rational thinking goes out the door when the party begins.

People have had brewing and fermenting alcoholic drinks since the beginning of time. Consumed in excess, alcohol is poisonous to the human system and is considered a drug. Nearly 100,000 Americans die each year as a result of alcohol abuse, and alcohol is a factor in more than half of the country's homicides, suicides and traffic accidents. Alcohol abuse also plays a role in many social and domestic problems.

The immediate physical effects of drinking range from mild mood changes to complete loss of coordination, vision, balance and speech is known as acute intoxication. Larger amounts of blood alcohol can impair brain function and cause unconsciousness and an extreme overdose can be fatal.

Poor nutrition goes hand-in-hand with heavy drinking and seniors who drink may be adding to their woes especially, those who live alone. Many of friends find it too difficult to prepare meals for themselves. Some of the people I know indulge in the cocktail hour and forego a proper meal thus weakening their immune system.

I have heard people say that they take vitamins and have plenty of exercise. They never say that they eat properly. There have been many times when I have witnessed golfers returning from their game and settle down with a gin and tonic. The 19th hole is a favorite watering spot. Many of these people would rather drink than eat.

One of the most difficult times I had was at the doctor's office after I had been sober for a year. I complained that I could not sleep and he began to prescribe a prescription for me. Panic set in and I had to admit that I was a recovering alcoholic. He was the first person outside of my family and AA group that I told of my addiction. He applauded my efforts and noted my chart. Now, I thought: "Wonderful, the news will be all over his office. The nurses will surely spread the news." I became paranoid. I could not look the nurse in the eye when leaving the office. One would think that I had committed murder. Since then, I have told my dentist, the surgeon that did a bypass on the arteries in my leg, and the other surgeon who repaired my shoulder.

Seniors who have otherwise been upright citizens and are recovering alcoholics will certainly suffer embarrassing situations, as I did. When I refuse alcohol at socials I did find it necessary to explain why I didn't drink. Casually, I would say that I was on medication that did not allow it, as good an excuse as any. However, one of my fellow travelers recently refused the wine being served at the service honoring the Jewish Sabbath by saying, "I don't drink. I'm an alcoholic!"

I am at odds with this issue. Should we be admitting to others outside of the AA program that we are recovering alcoholics? Perhaps, if we do, the message will spread more quickly than it has to this point.

Recently, one of my daughter-in-law's friends complained to her, that her mother had a problem with alcohol. It was then that my daughter-in law told her about me. If I had been new to the program I might have been upset that my alcoholism was being discussed, but now I was happy to be able to help someone else.

The friend's mother was definitely a senior. She was educated and had worked for years as a chemist. Certainly she was bright and knew the dangers of alcohol, but she wouldn't and couldn't stop drinking. She was in complete denial. She could not classify herself as an alcoholic even though she consumed her daily four or five martinis. She was alienating her family and literally killing herself. Part of her problem was loneliness as it is with so many seniors who suddenly find themselves alone after having shared forty or fifty years with a mate. They no longer have anyone to care for, no more meals to make, no more mutual dates to keep. They are alone, or think they are. They suffer nightmares about relying upon their children or friends. They do not want to be criticized, told how or where to live or how to lead their lives and they rebel. I know one woman who has been widowed for twelve years and she talks about her widowhood as if it happened yesterday. She drinks and will not give up the ghost.

The people who tell me about their parent or parents' problem drinking and ask for my advice I always suggest that they have their parent call me. When I do speak with the person, the first thing I hear is the denial. I suggest meeting for coffee so that we can discuss the problem, if there is one. The people who are in denial will not accept my offer and I do not push the issue. The one or two people who have met with me, I am sad to say that, they could not accept going to AA. For those people had mental blocks and said that AA was not for Jewish people.

Somewhere in the Bible it talks about being "stiffed necked." Imagine having a support system and not taking advantage of it. I can understand the stigma that AA holds. For years it was known as a place for drunks and low-lifes, a bad rumor that must have been spread by unknowing persons. One just has to look at the number of celebrities and well-known people who have publicly related their stories. Even, our President, George Bush has admitted that he is a recovering alcoholic. If our rabbis would accept the issue and pursue it, perhaps more Jewish people would be able to admit to being an alcoholic or drug addict and take their condition seriously.

AA meetings are held in every country, every city and every town, all over the world. I have attended meetings in

Israel, Alaska, Thailand, Hong Kong, England and the United States. I have even been to a meeting while on a cruise. A little known fact is, if you are on a plane and feel the urge to drink when that beverage cart goes by, you can ask the stewardess to announce a message asking if there is a friend of Bill Wilson on board. Bill Wilson is the name of the man responsible for the formation of AA. Every alcoholic knows the name and it is an SOS for help.

Although, I am Jewish I do enter a church willingly for a meeting. In Israel I attended meetings in a bomb shelter.

There are not many churches in Israel and synagogues do not open their doors for AA. Bomb shelters—during peaceful times—are available. I will admit that it quite an eerie feeling to walk down into the underground shelter.

I have learned that the more isolated a place is, for whatever reason, the more alcoholics there are. Alaska probably ranks very high on the list. Long winters, ice and snow most of the time can lead to isolation and loneliness, followed by substance abuse. Martha's Vineyard was another location where alcoholism seemed to be the outstanding recreation and a great place to meet the celebrities that are charter members of AA.

In Hong Kong and Thailand most of the people at the AA meetings were English speaking foreigners; Embassy members, dignitaries, and hotel employees. Basically, people who were far from their families and home and the cocktail hour had become their major source of social integration.

Usually, I do not require a meeting when I am traveling

but I have a natural curiosity about AA in other parts of the world. It is easy to find the meetings. The local telephone directory actually will list Alcoholics Anonymous.

Chapter XXI

To say the least, I am—at best—a grateful recovering alcoholic. I would have to say that I am most grateful because I can enjoy my children and six grandchildren. The very thought of being a falling down, drunken grandmother is gross. Or a grandmother that gets on the phone and drunkenly babbles. I know those grandmothers and grandfathers and it is disgusting.

A gigantic worry that I had was warning my grandchildren about the possibility of inheriting the alcoholic gene. I hear too many young people at meetings say, "I am a cross addicted alcoholic." That means that they do drugs and alcohol. I can easily imagine the frustration, the pain, and the resignation that their parents are experiencing.

Early on in the program I told my older grandchildren, who were fourteen and fifteen at the time, that I was an alcoholic. I also told them about my father and grandfathers. I explained the possibility of the alcoholic gene. I do not know how much they understood. Now I have grandchildren between the ages of 20 and 5 years old. Recently, I heard two of them say, "When E… is Bat Mitzvah I will be able to drink." It seems that they can hardly wait for the day.

My eldest granddaughter attends college and I know she socially drinks but I also know that she likes it. I just pray that she doesn't like it too much. I know that there a drinking law in New York State, but I also know that this girl is underage, yet, no one questions her status when she is out with her friends, in a college town, drinking. I can only rely on her good judgment in order to maintain my peace of mind.

I believe that I am now a realistic person and I want to face the present issues in our society. Two of the biggest issues at hand are drugs and alcohol. We give sex education in the schools, why not a program for substance abuse? The schools do have speakers that visit and lecture but it is not enough. The glory stories that are told about the drugs: Ecstasy, Cocaine, Hash, Speed, Angel Dust, LSD, Crack and Booze, (did I leave anything out?) can only help to fuel an imaginative, young person's mind. Social, parental, and school pressures might induce a boy or girl to sample one of the above. None of those substances are difficult to obtain in today's marketplace. I have been assured by the young people who attend meetings that anything is available.

My favorite meeting, which I consider my home group, is at a church near to my home. Not to long ago, a young man attended our meeting. He announced that he was cross addicted and was twenty years old. He had gotten a citation for driving while intoxicated and was at the mercy of his parents and friends to transport him. The judge at the hearing for his DUI also ordered him to attend AA meetings. He told his story and it was pitiful.

Unfortunately, he did not have a good relationship with his parents. Since the age of twelve he had been drinking and smoking marijuana. He had been put on probation from school so his family withdrew him from the public school system and sent him to private school. He explained how his mother and father were constantly working, involved in their own lives, never having time to talk to him. When he did get into trouble all they could do was scream at him for upsetting their lives. When he received the DUI it was the last straw. Now, he was to be sent to a school far away from home so that he could not be in touch with his friends, who his parents thought were a bad influence on him. He was so young and so sad. I asked him if he had a grandmother. He said that he had. I told him to visit her and that I was sure that she would be very happy to hear from her. His last remark was, "My grandmother is an alcoholic." As he left the meeting and was putting on his coat, I couldn't help but notice the Jewish Star hanging from a gold chain around his neck.

From time to time, I still talk to my grandchildren about my addiction and the meetings that I attend. I did discuss with one of the girls about writing this book and whether I should use my own name. I wanted to know if it would embarrass her. She said, "Softah, I am very proud of you and I want you to use your real name." So I have.

Chapter XXII

With all of the problems, I have the distinct feeling that our Jewish leaders are deserting us. I'm waiting for one rabbi to give a sermon: Jews and Booze. Perhaps, it will induce other Jewish leaders to do the same.

When I do attend religious services I do not feel the same spirituality that I find at an ordinary AA meeting. The sermons at the temple usually leave me wanting something more. I am always in admiration of the atmosphere and elated at the sight of the Torah and Scrolls. I delight in reading the biblical stories and I always find new information. But I am left cold with the rabbi's message and I come away with little satisfaction.

At an AA meeting the messages are real. I can identify with the stories that are told and I come away with the feeling of camaraderie.

In AA religion is not important but faith in a higher power is very important. I relate both religiously and spiritually.

Fortunately, I grew up in a family that believed in charity. We had the little blue and white Tzedakah box (box for collecting coins to be donated to charity) in the cupboard. My family was always aware of people in need and shared whatever little they had. It was during the Depression when one of my father's friends, a fireman, had an accident while fighting a fire and could not work that my father gave him enough money to see his family through the ordeal. I don't know where my father was able to accumulate the money, but from that time on I never saw the diamond stickpin that he always wore again. I can only suppose that he pawned it to give his friend the money.

My father certainly lived his life as a righteous Jew, except for his susceptibility to drink. As in AA, Judaism instructs us admit our sins, to show regret and to promise not to repeat the sins. My father should have admitted to his alcoholism but it was beyond him.

I look towards my higher power for help. I realize that if I am poor of spirit I have nothing. I am grateful for my religion because the Torah gives me the paths to follow and maintain my spirituality. If I were not Jewish, I do not know what religion I would lean to, if any. I have listened to the stories of my Catholic friends, but I cannot find any more redemption in their religion than I can in mine.

When I do attend services I wait for the Kaddish (a prayer for the dead) and visualize my mother, father and brother. I need the connection to bring additional peace to my soul.

My higher power, my spirituality, and meditation allow me to see my soul standing right next to me. Call it transcendental meditation, if you will. I like the feeling of my shadow standing nearby. I can enjoy great peace and a sense of well being. When I recall how frantically I had lived, I cannot believe that I am the same person as I am now.

Of course, I still have the same personality. I am naturally hyper and have high energy. I still want music and I revel in hearing and telling jokes. Cooking is a favorite hobby. I have collected recipes from all of the places I have lived and traveled to see. Baking unusual breads is a special challenge. From time to time I will write and submit a food article to a magazine. Several have found their way to being published and I have instant gratification. I have been working on a cookbook and hopefully, it will become a reality. Life is fun!

I always knew life was fun but while I was drinking I couldn't really enjoy it. Life only became durable when I stopped denying my alcoholism and admitted that I was an alcoholic. That's the first step.

It all happened suddenly and I'm told that it was due to fact that I had hit bottom with nowhere to go. We all know that a new beginning is difficult. Whether we are marrying, starting a new job, or moving to a new location, beginning is tough. I discovered that when I became sober I was starting a new way of life, and I was ready.

Well into my sobriety I realized that I didn't hear the whispering among my sober friends: "Too bad she's an alcoholic."

I did receive the frank talk, though: "You're no fun any more now that you don't drink!"

I thought I was fun! Of course, I had to accept where

the remarks were coming from.

Chapter XXIII

There are times when we have to face overwhelming challenges and by having fragile personalities it can be difficult. I have learned that the important thing is not to look back, but rather into the future. I believe that we do have the ability to tap into the future if we open the door and do our best. When we do, we will find ourselves succeeding beyond our wildest dreams. With the help of my higher power I can accomplish more than I could by going at it alone.

However, I know that I have to make the first move even if it's just a little push to bring down God's blessing into my life.

People sometimes engage in self-destructive behavior, rejecting assistance that others may offer. The kindest and most loving thing family and friends can do is to intervene with someone who is suffering. Years ago intervention once was used for alcohol abusers. Now, it is used for compulsive gamblers, those having eating disorders, and other self-destructive behavior. Help on the ways of intervention can be found at Al-ANON and can be reached by phoning: 1-888-4Alanon. If the problem is with a teenager there is a group known as Alateen and associated with Al-ANON.

Intervention is not always done by people. Sometimes, a mysterious power intervenes. I am reminded of the story that I heard at a meeting: A very tall, handsome man stood at a meeting and said, "I'm Fred and I'm an alcoholic.... I was in total despair. My life was ruined. I was emotionally bankrupt and on a miserable rainy day, decided to commit suicide. I went into the garage and hooked a hose up to the exhaust pipe and turned on the engine. I opened the door of the car and sat comfortably in the backseat waiting and expecting to die. At that moment the phone in the kitchen began to ring, and would not give up. I turned off the motor and went to answer the phone, thinking death can wait. The call was from my neighbor telling me that her kitchen was flooded and she did not know where the water turn off valve was. Could I possibly come and help. I did, and then sat comfortably in her kitchen listening to her tales of woe. By the time I left, the rain had stopped, the sun was shining and I would swear that I saw a rainbow. Going back home I opened the garage doors to let the fumes evaporate, stored the hose and forgot about killing myself. I showered and dressed and went to a meeting. Thank you God, and thank you everyone."

With that, he sat. Everyone stood and applauded. Chills ran up and down my spine. I had listened to the story of a miracle.

Miracles happen every day. I believe that my life has been saved and blessed by a miracle. There is a part in the

Peter Pan story when Wendy tells everyone to clap their hands if they believe in fairies. I am asking everyone to clap their hands if they believe in angels and miracles.

Clap those hands!

Printed in the United States
1160600001B/215